# Slimline Secrets

## *Escape* from Depression

The Complete, Step-by-step Blueprint for Getting Better

David M Hinds

Published by SLIMLINE SECRETS UK

COPYRIGHT © 2011 David M Hinds

David M Hinds asserts the moral right to be identified as the author of this work

Series Editor: Wanda Whiteley

A catalogue record for this book, deposited with the British Library on June 8$^{th}$ 2011, is available for public scrutiny

ISBN 978-0-9569151-0-8

Printed and bound by
Intype Libra Limited, London

1 3 5 7 9 10 8 6 4 2

All rights reserved. No part of this publication may be reproduced, stored in a retrieval system, or transmitted, in any form or by any means, electronic, mechanical, photocopying, recording or otherwise, without the prior permission of the publishers.

## SLIMLINE SECRETS SERIES

### NEW TITLES

Love
Success
Quit Smoking
Get Well Soon
Effective Complaining
Bouncing Back from Failure

### By David M Hinds

*Slimline Secrets* have the distinction of being the first books that are great to read on a mobile phone. One page fits the screen of the new generation Android cell phones with no scrolling.

## PUBLISHING FORMAT

The *Slimline Secrets* motivational self-help series of mini-books is also published in:

- App download for new generation
- Android mobile phones
- App download for iPhone
- App download for BlackBerry
- e-Book for iPad
- e-Book for Kindle
- e-Book for eReader

It is the publisher's policy to give download customers the same rights to browse before purchase as retail customers in a bookshop. The first 25 pages of each title may be downloaded free of charge. We hope you enjoy and benefit greatly from *Slimline Secrets*.

What other dungeon is as dark as one's own heart! What jailer as inexorable as one's self!

Nathaniel Hawthorne (1804—64)
*The House of the Seven Gables*

## ABOUT THE AUTHOR

David M Hinds is a stress management consultant who made his first £1million by franchising his award-winning consultancy in Milton Keynes.

In 1995 David lost everything with the onset of two strokes. From his hospital bed, he adapted stress management techniques to make the best recovery available.

As a result of his stroke experiences and the surgical reconstruction of the blood flow to his brain, David has to break tasks down into simple steps. *Slimline Secrets*—the first book that's great to read on a new generation mobile phone screen—is the result.

One simple fail-safe step forward at a time is David's mantra in therapy. In *Slimline Secrets*, overburdening chapters are scrapped in favour of single theme double-page-spreads. These books are overflowing with compassion, stimulating ideas, and rock-solid solutions for readers braving the insecurities of change in search of a better life.

David's previous books were published in the UK by HarperCollins, and Hodder. His first book was featured on ITV's THIS MORNING programme with Richard and Judy, and Channel 5 News. He is the founder of *Slimline Secrets* and in 2011 his fledgling publishing company was featured in the BBC's Dragons' Den.

To my third and final wife, Tatiana, and to my son, Jason, and my daughters, Johanna and Danielle together with my friends—*past and present*—and the few who have been with me all along through adventure and misadventure.

To you and my readers I offer the perceived wisdom of a thousand bloopers and the handful of hard-won successes that make everything so wonderfully worthwhile. Bless you all!

Wednesday, 8th June 2011

## CONTENTS

| | | |
|---|---|---|
| | Introduction | 13 |
| 01 | Step one: tick the box | 14 |
| 02 | Functioning on autopilot | 16 |
| 03 | I cannot help myself | 18 |
| 04 | What can the doctor do? | 20 |
| 05 | The spotlight of your mind | 22 |
| 06 | Hope | 24 |
| 07 | Clinical depression | 26 |
| 08 | 'You mean I don't have to'... | 28 |
| 09 | Why me? | 30 |
| 10 | Bitter thoughts | 32 |
| 11 | Anxiety | 34 |
| 12 | Losing in love | 36 |
| 13 | Aversion therapy | 38 |
| 14 | Career crash | 40 |
| 15 | Excess alcohol | 42 |
| 16 | All alone? | 44 |
| 17 | Failure | 46 |
| 18 | Dominant personalities | 48 |
| 19 | Dominant personality recall | 50 |

| | | |
|---|---|---|
| 20 | Debt, despondency and death | 52 |
| 21 | Is this your child? | 54 |
| 22 | Teen depression | 56 |
| 23 | Laughter | 58 |
| 24 | Passion | 60 |
| 25 | Passion graphic | 62 |
| 26 | Suicide | 64 |
| 27 | Suicidal tendencies | 66 |
| 28 | Seasonal affective disorder | 68 |
| 29 | Internet blues | 70 |
| 30 | 'Baby blues'/postnatal… | 72 |
| 31 | I'm a man: we don't do… | 74 |
| 32 | Depression in terminal illness | 76 |
| 33 | Anger | 78 |
| 34 | Happiness | 80 |
| 35 | Retired early, on the scrap… | 82 |
| 36 | Specialist intervention | 84 |
| 37 | McDavid & Burger-queen | 86 |
| 38 | The healthy eating pyramid | 88 |
| 39 | Maslow's hierarchy of needs | 90 |
| 40 | Training your mind | 92 |
| 41 | Dumping excess baggage | 94 |

| | | |
|---|---|---|
| 42 | Thought-stopping strategies | 96 |
| 43 | Desperation or inspiration? | 98 |
| 44 | Neutralising anger | 100 |
| 45 | Taming fear | 102 |
| 46 | Getting active | 104 |
| 47 | Staying active | 106 |
| 48 | Quality sleep | 108 |
| 49 | Self-esteem | 110 |
| 50 | Greater self-esteem | 112 |
| 51 | Default settings of your mind | 114 |
| 52 | D-thoughts | 116 |
| 53 | Revised default settings/mind | 118 |
| 54 | SS30 | 120 |
| 55 | Therapeutic thoughts | 122 |
| 56 | The talking therapies | 124 |
| 57 | The ultimate challenge... | 126 |
| 58 | Forgiveness: preparing for it | 128 |
| 59 | Forgiveness: what if I'm not... | 130 |
| 60 | Forgiveness: thinking about it | 132 |
| 61 | Forgiveness: the principles | 134 |
| 62 | Forgiveness: doing it! | 136 |
| 63 | Swimming with dolphins | 138 |

| | | |
|---|---|---|
| 64 | Music therapy | 140 |
| 65 | Dance therapy | 142 |
| 66 | Pet therapy | 144 |
| 67 | Massage | 146 |
| 68 | Sex in depression | 148 |
| 69 | Hot baths and mind games | 150 |
| 70 | A purpose in life | 152 |
| 71 | Realizing your purpose | 154 |
| 72 | Clarifying your purpose | 156 |
| 72 | Committing... | 158 |
| 74 | Love | 160 |
| 75 | Enjoying the moment | 162 |
| 76 | Highlighting | 164 |
| 77 | The door is open... | 166 |
| 78 | My resolution | 167 |
| | The farewell quotation | 168 |
| | New/forthcoming titles | 169 |

## INTRODUCTION

This book is for people who are depressed. It is written from the depressed person's point of view but provides insights and information for loved ones, carers, family and friends.

Let's assume you are depressed and need help. What you want is *release*: escape from your all-consuming feelings of misery, hopelessness and isolation. You have just picked up the book that is going to make this happen! Life is going to get better and you will have peace of mind.

We start with an invitation to take the first step towards recognizing, identifying and gaining release from your condition. One tick is all I ask. No matter how depressed you are right now, you can do it. Let's tick the box.

## STEP ONE: TICK THE BOX

Are you depressed? If so, how depressed are you?
Let's begin to find out...
In order to ascertain the best and safest way forward, please decide how depressed you are on a scale of 0—5.
Your choice should reflect how you have been feeling generally over the last couple of weeks. Don't worry if your selection is not quite right. Give yourself permission to adopt a trial and error approach. We can always put things right later when we understand more about your prevailing mood, your circumstances, your feelings, your psychological makeup and the overall structure of your thinking patterns.

<u>THE BOTTOM LINE</u>
Get your pen out.

Escape from Depression / 15

## STEP ONE: TICK THE BOX

- [ ] (0) Not Depressed
- [ ] (1) Mildly Depressed
- [ ] (2) Rather Depressed
- [ ] (3) Very Depressed
- [ ] (4) Extreme Highs & Lows
- [ ] (5) Suicidal Thoughts

Well done! You've started.
Not long now before we begin to mastermind your escape from depression.

## FUNCTIONING ON AUTOPILOT

O for a life of sensations rather than of thoughts!

John Keats (1795—1821)
English Romantic Poet

## **FUNCTIONING ON AUTOPILOT**

As depression creeps up on us by stealth and silently takes us over, many of us soldier on, denying to ourselves and to others that anything's wrong. We battle on as best we can, oblivious to the reality that the joy of life is gradually being squeezed out of us.

In order for our condition to be classified as depression in medical terms, there needs to be clear evidence of a lowering of mood. This lowered mood may vary in intensity throughout the day but would normally prevent sufferers from being cheered up by their family or friends. This is the major distinction between being sad and suffering depression. On the basis of this distinction, visit your GP if necessary.

### THE BOTTOM LINE
In time the pilot will resume control.

## I CANNOT HELP MYSELF

The mind is its own place, and in itself can make heaven of Hell, a hell of Heaven.

> John Milton (1608—1674)
> *Paradise Lost*

## I CANNOT HELP MYSELF

You already have done: you ticked the box to get started and you're reading the book. That's a milestone for someone who is depressed. You are going to be OK.

You are not alone. I have been where you are now. I will write for you and you will read for me. The mere fact that you are here with me now—sharing my experiences and reading this book—means that deep down you possess a courageous and determined streak that will help pull you through, even though you may be facing your darkest hour right now. Someday soon I promise you will have the opportunity to escape from depression and enjoy your life.

### THE BOTTOM LINE

Depression, though soul-destroying and misunderstood, is never permanent.

## WHAT CAN THE DOCTOR DO?

Healing is a matter of time,
But it is sometimes also a matter of opportunity.

Hippocrates (460—377 BC)
Ancient Greek physician

## WHAT CAN THE DOCTOR DO?

Your GP can establish whether or not you need specialist treatment. If you ticked boxes 3—5, you should visit your GP. Some forms of depression need to be diagnosed and treated by a medical practitioner. This book will help you in any event, but I am a great believer in accurate diagnosis.

If you are very depressed and have yet to visit your GP, you are probably struggling on in bewildered isolation under the mistaken impression that your troubles are yours alone.

Do visit your GP and mention your main worries and symptoms at the outset. If you are feeling pretty grim, say so. If you don't, you may never find out how sympathetic, supportive, and knowledgeable your GP can be.

### THE BOTTOM LINE
Consult the professionals.

## THE SPOTLIGHT OF YOUR MIND

Whether you believe you can or can't, *you're right*.

Henry Ford (1863—1947)
Founder of the Ford Motor Company

## THE SPOTLIGHT OF YOUR MIND

The seat of all thought and memory is your mind. This centre of consciousness works rather like a spotlight of awareness, highlighting some areas of your immediate existence, while ignoring others. What you pay attention to and how you respond is determined largely by what matters to you most in any given situation.

If you know what you want in life and imprint that vision repeatedly on your mind, that spotlight of awareness will become trained and tuned to highlight aspects of your life that will enable you to get what you want.

Similarly, if you dwell on how depressing your life is, that same spotlight of awareness will focus on reasons galore to confirm depression.

THE BOTTOM LINE
Spotlight the good things.

## HOPE

Once you choose hope,
anything's possible.

*Superman* star Christopher Reeve, American actor, film director and producer who was paralysed when he broke his neck after being thrown from a horse in 1995; the year I suffered two paralysing strokes from which I recovered over a period of 4 years.

## HOPE

Depression means different things to different people but if you are the unfortunate soul trapped in the prison of your mind, this condition has a singular and disagreeable manifestation for you. In your misery and isolation, please bear in mind that some of the greatest, most talented individuals in history have suffered from depression so your worth as a human being is not devalued.

The secret of getting better from all forms of depressive illness is revised thinking. To make this realizable for everyone, from a teenager to a pensioner, I have packaged the process into easy stages as we progress through the book. All I ask of you at this point is hope: hope for recovery, *total recovery*.

THE BOTTOM LINE

Without hope life is empty.

## **CLINICAL DEPRESSION**

In the real dark night of the soul it is always three o'clock in the morning.

F. Scott Fitzgerald (1896—1940)
*The Crack-up*

## CLINICAL DEPRESSION

Clinical depression adversely affects our thought patterns and mood, our feelings, our energy levels and our overall ability to function normally, as well as our physical wellbeing. It is most certainly not just a matter of feeling 'blue' or 'under the weather'. It is more intense than feeling sad or experiencing grief and, most serious of all, there is a high incidence of suicide amongst the clinically depressed. A doctor's diagnosis is vital.

Clinical depression is a tragedy by any standards, but much good can come out of it if we are persuaded to put right what is wrong in our lives.

<u>THE BOTTOM LINE</u>

You are at the starting line. Well done!

## 'YOU MEAN I DON'T HAVE TO FEEL LIKE THIS'

I thought I had just woken up from a terrible nightmare, but then I realized that I didn't dream last night.

Guest C. EMMY
Depression.about.com website

## 'YOU MEAN I DON'T HAVE TO FEEL LIKE THIS'

With the major advances in medicine today and our greater understanding of brain chemistry and therapy for the mind, it is no longer necessary to wait for depression to lift. You can take simple steps to start the process. The first step is to visit your GP and get the professionals working for you.

Horror stories of antidepressant drugs and electric shock treatments flood to mind perhaps? Fear not, these days your local GP has a range of treatments at their disposal, including 'talking treatments'. These treatments explore the origins and the core issues of your depression. We can deal with your concerns as we progress through the book.

### THE BOTTOM LINE
You decide how you want to feel.

## WHY ME?

What lies behind us, and what lies
before us are tiny matters,
compared to what lies within us.

Ralph Waldo Emerson (1803—82)
American lecturer, essayist and poet

## WHY ME?

There is a genetic predisposition to some forms of depression, particularly those that recur. People who have a greater biological sensitivity to depression are more likely to switch into depressed states of mind because something goes wrong with the way that neurochemicals are produced and used in the brain. This malfunction is believed to be due to our genes. There is no mileage in blaming others. This is the surest way to stay in depression. In blaming one or other of our parents or anyone else involved in our upbringing—*including ourselves*—we negate our ability to help ourselves. The future is decided not by our genes, but to a great extent by our current thinking and actions.

### THE BOTTOM LINE

Our thoughts determine our future.

## BITTER THOUGHTS

If we could read the secret history of our enemies, we should find in each man's life sorrow and suffering enough to disarm hostility.

Henry Wadsworth Longfellow
(1807—82)
*Driftwood*

## BITTER THOUGHTS

Let's examine our own bitter thoughts and observe how we are keeping our suffering alive, red-hot and self-destructive.

All too often we perpetuate our pain by keeping it the focus of our thoughts, replaying our hurts over and over again in our minds, magnifying injustices and vilifying the offender. We add to our discomfort by being overly sensitive, overreacting to minor irritations and temporary setbacks. How many of us have punished ourselves time and time again by taking things too personally?

If you recognize yourself here, be kinder to yourself. Challenge and neutralize these bitter thoughts. You will find techniques to accomplish this later.

### THE BOTTOM LINE
Forgive and forget.

## ANXIETY

*In the eyes of the advertising industry…*

The most desirable mental state for a potential consumer is a kind of free-floating anxiety and depression combined with a nice collection of unrealistic goals and desires.

The New York Review of Books
2$^{nd}$ June 1983

## ANXIETY

Anxiety, the precursor to depression, can be a mental bully, best understood if we imagine an old-fashioned cassette player. The reel on the left of the cassette has a recording of your past anxieties and the other reel, which represents your future, has only blank tape because you have yet to live and record the rest of your life. Where the tape goes through the tape head is where you are in life now—depressed.

If you suffer from panic attacks or depression, you may have a tendency to rake up the past (replay the tape through the tape head of your mind) and relive unhappy events and past foul-ups.

If this sounds like you, we have some unfinished business later in the book.

### THE BOTTOM LINE

Anxiety is fear spread thin and wide.

## LOSING IN LOVE

There are two tragedies in life.
One is to lose your heart's desire.
The other is to gain it.

George Bernard Shaw (1856—1950)
*Man and Superman*

## LOSING IN LOVE

Losing in love hurts like hell and is almost guaranteed to induce anger, disbelief, depression and despair. You may feel you will never love, or be loved again. You will, of course, but you cannot be expected to believe this just yet.

This is a time when you really need the comfort and support of family and friends. If you don't have family or friends to turn to (and even if you do), I'll give you a simple technique over the page that will definitely help to get the offending ex-lover out of your mind. It sounds crazy, but it has never once failed to work if applied correctly in all my years of seeing one-to-one clients in my stress management consultancy.

<u>THE BOTTOM LINE</u>

Life can be a bitch, but tomorrow may be a peach

## AVERSION THERAPY

How can I forget you when you are
always on my mind?
How can I not want you when you are
all I want inside?
How can I let you go when I can't see
us apart?
How can I not love you when you
control my heart?

Author Unknown
from the poemslovers.com website
19th May, 2011

## AVERSION THERAPY

Please read the previous *Losing in love* section before proceeding with aversion therapy. Losing in love hurts so I have no qualms about introducing you to more pain in the form of a rubber band to be worn around your wrist at all times, day and night. Keep it there until all thoughts of your ex are eradicated from mind.

Make sure the rubber band fits loosely enough not to restrict circulation, but snugly enough so it won't fall off. Every time you think of your ex, snap the band! Snap it firmly enough so that it stings, but not hard enough to leave welts on your wrist. Soon, you'll forget him/her! Make no mistake: the humble rubber band is one of the big guns of stress management. Aversion therapy works. Ouch!

### THE BOTTOM LINE
Snap the band, forget the ex.

## CAREER CRASH

It's a recession when your neighbour loses his job;
it's a depression when you lose yours.

Henry S Truman (1884-1972)
33rd President of the United States

## CAREER CRASH

Losing your job or experiencing a career crash can be a shattering experience. For many, however, once the initial shock has worn off, it can be a great (forced, unexpected, probably inconvenient, but nevertheless there for the taking) opportunity to get a better job, study, work overseas, start a business or work from home.

How you react depends on your attitude. And your attitude is a topic we will be visiting later. Is the treasure trove half empty, or half full?

In 1995, I lost everything: my health, my business and my independence. This bolt from the blue forced me to review my life and change. I am happier and wiser now because of this tragedy.

### THE BOTTOM LINE
Attitude is everything.

## EXCESS ALCOHOL

Of course you can get a quart into a pint pot
— you can get a couple of gallons in if you stay until closing time.

Patrick Skene Catling
British children's author

## EXCESS ALCOHOL

Excessive drinking actually leads to depression more often than it is a symptom of depression. If you have difficulty cutting down or knowing when to stop, total abstinence may be the only sustainable option. Many former alcoholics have found happiness without booze, but not before they recognized they had a problem and took action. Alcoholics lie to themselves!

In view of a report by doctors that many patients questioned about their drinking habits underestimate their alcohol consumption by as much as 50%, I urge you to avoid the temptation of using alcohol as a means of drowning your sorrows or lifting your spirits.

### THE BOTTOM LINE
You can be happy without booze.

## All ALONE?

Maybe love won't let you down.
All of your failures are training
grounds and just as your back is
turned you'll be surprised... as your
solitude subsides.

Author Unknown
From the thinkexist.com website
20th May, 2011

## ALL ALONE?

Of all the symptoms of depression, the sense of being isolated and cut off from the rest of humanity must surely be the cruellest. It impacts savagely on friends and loved ones of the depressed person as well because they often feel shut out and their efforts to help are shunned.

On the other hand, all the lonely people who John Lennon and Paul McCartney were referring to in their song 'Eleanor Rigby' were surely not all depressed all of the time?

If you are genuinely all alone and in need of company or a loving partner, the only way to make it happen is to put yourself out there where the action is. If you prefer, you could start online.

### THE BOTTOM LINE
Never give up on love.

## FAILURE

Far better it is to dare mighty things, to win glorious triumphs, even though chequered by failure, than to rank with those poor spirits who neither enjoy much nor suffer much, because they live in the grey twilight that knows no victory or defeat.

Theodore Roosevelt (1858—1919)
26th President of the United States

## FAILURE

Do you, in common with most depressed people, live much of your life in the past? Do you dwell on mistakes, turning them over in your mind as if you were stuck in a time warp? One of the most disabling beliefs that many of us have is that the person we were yesterday is the person we must be today, tomorrow and for evermore.

This ridiculous belief is about as watertight as the Titanic. In fact, success often follows hard on the heels of failure, but the rewards of persistence are only available to those who are prepared to pick themselves up, learn from their mistakes, and carry on trying. Failure is a magnificent teacher: she is not a kind one, but she is effective.

### THE BOTTOM LINE

Failure is a detour en-route to success.

## DOMINANT PERSONALITIES

*If I were your wife I would poison your coffee.*

Nancy, Viscountess Astor
(1879—1964)
Society hostess, women's rights activist and the first woman MP to sit in the British House of Commons

*If I were your husband I would drink it.*

Winston Churchill (1874—1965)
2nd World War British Prime Minister

## DOMINANT PERSONALITIES

Some people with bouts of recurring depression are adversely affected by a dominant personality (DP). This could be the person they are in a relationship with, a family member, or anyone—*dead or alive*—in authority from their past.

It is very much in the interest of the depressed person to identify the DP in their life in order to eliminate any adverse influence. It is worth noting that many people live happy lives with dominant personalities and they are not, by virtue of their DP status, bad people.

Some people, however, are adversely affected and become depressed. If this sounds like you, I will take you through a process of DP recall overleaf.

### THE BOTTOM LINE

Review the status of your relationship.

## DOMINANT PERSONALITY RECALL

This exercise is intrinsically linked to the previous section: DOMININANT PERSONALITIES.

**Step 1**: Sit down with pen and paper.

**Step 2**: Think! Remind yourself who are (and have been) the influential people in your life from now back into childhood.

**Step 3**: The process of elimination—Make a complete list of all the people who have opposed you in a major way, commencing with the most recent opposition, continuing right back to childhood. It could be that your list will include someone who is now dead.

**Step 4**: Go through the list several times deleting only one name at a time, commencing with the least influential.

**Step 5**: Repeat the process until *only one name* remains. Now you should be left with the DP who may be affecting you: the significant one (SDP).

## DOMINANT PERSONALITY RECALL

**Step 6**: Dealing with the problem once identified. Sometimes the SDP is no longer present in your life; an overly strict parent or an institutional care-worker, etc. Tell yourself *emphatically* this person no longer has the right to influence you. Say it like you mean it. Say it again! Reclaim your life!
If the SDP is currently part of your life, you must make beneficial changes to the nature or status of the relationship in order to escape from depression. Hopefully, if you are romantically attached or professionally connected to the SDP, they will respond positively to your sensitivities in future. Otherwise, you would be advised to consider your options.

THE BOTTOM LINE

Your life is your life, nobody else's.

## DEBT, DESPONDENCY AND DEATH

He who has never hoped can never despair.

George Bernard Shaw (1856—1950)
*Caesar and Cleopatra*

## DEBT, DESPONDENCY AND DEATH

Debt and money worries are a major cause of stress and depression, and insufficient funds have wrecked many beautiful relationships and lives. But now there are free helplines and safety nets for those seeking help. Call! Call!

Life for the clinically depressed and despondent person can seem like a life sentence of regret: regret for lost opportunities and the mistakes of the past. Clinical depression needs medical supervision. If you cannot see the way forward, consult your GP. Seek help!

Grief, a natural human reaction to loss, is a process of adaption: alarm, shock, denial, anger, guilt, acceptance and adjustment. Time is the great healer.

### THE BOTTOM LINE

This is when friends show their worth.

## IS THIS YOUR CHILD?

Children begin by loving their parents;
after a time they judge them;
rarely, if ever, do they forgive them.

Oscar Wilde (1854—1900)
*A Woman of No Importance*

## IS THIS YOUR CHILD?

My childhood got off to a flying start but grounded at the age of eight when my parents clashed. I have fond pre-school memories of *Listen with Mother* on BBC radio and great affection for my infant schooldays when I learnt to read. I was enchanted by words and stories. The best defence against depression that parents can give their offspring is to provide a stable and loving environment and to encourage them to develop resilience in life. Resilient children recover more quickly from frustration, disappointment and change. They are less likely to become overwhelmed by the challenges of childhood, adolescence, and then adulthood, less likely to succumb to depression.

### THE BOTTOM LINE
Every child deserves a happy childhood

## TEEN DEPRESSION

We do not see things as they are.
We see them as we are.

*The Talmud* (c. AD 500)

## TEEN DEPRESSION

Depressed teenagers need to have their feelings acknowledged and taken seriously. They need to be able to express their feelings as they feel them. It is not helpful to tell a depressed teenager to snap out of it. Nobody stays depressed if they can help it. It is the most empty, joyless existence imaginable.

Young people in their teens often assess their predicament, their prospects and their self-worth inaccurately. Simply arranging for an app download of this book or placing a copy of the paperback version in an appropriate place can do wonders should they decide to read it. Your role as parent, guardian, friend or trusted mentor is to tempt them out of isolation by engaging their interest.

THE BOTTOM LINE
A wise and trusted mentor is invaluable.

## LAUGHTER

Men will confess to treason, murder, arson, false teeth or a wig. How many of them will own up to a lack of humour?

Frank Moore Colby
American literary critic, editor and essayist

## LAUGHTER

Laughter raises our spirits and brings relief from pain by releasing endorphins—the body's natural painkillers—into the bloodstream. It exercises the lungs and tones the entire cardiovascular system, stimulating blood cells and antibodies. A good laugh can defuse tension, relieve stress, elevate mood and draw the sting from the agonies of life. Practise or *develop* your sense of humour and depression will eventually subside. *Think*! What can make you chuckle... a DVD, a picture, a memory? Bring it on!

### THE BOTTOM LINE
Laughter is medicine for body and soul.

## PASSION

If there is no passion in your life,
then have you really lived?
Find your passion, whatever it may be.
Become it, and let it become you and
you will find great things happen for
you, to you and because of you.

T. Alan Armstrong
American Editor

## PASSION

Passion is the most powerful human force in the world after love and survival. Passion has the power to sweep away depression by overwhelming it with lust and anticipation for something meaningful you desire and need that is absent from your life right now.

What is it? Do you want to paint or write or move or change your job? Do you want to start a business, a relationship, a charity; say 'sorry' to someone or appear on TV? Any of these things are possible if you want it enough.

Think about it; *keep thinking until you find the answer*. Then fill out the form that follows. I've included a spare in case you're reading this book with a friend.

### THE BOTTOM LINE

Passion will overpower depression.

62 / *Slimline Secrets*

## PASSION GRAPHIC

My name is

..................................................

My ultimate goal in life is

..................................................

..................................................

..................................................

My timetable for achieving this is

..................................................

..................................................

My feelings when I achieve success?

..................................................

..................................................

## PASSION GRAPHIC

My name is

..................................................

My ultimate goal in life is

..................................................

..................................................

..................................................

My timetable for achieving this is

..................................................

..................................................

My feelings when I achieve success?

..................................................

..................................................

## SUICIDE

When your principles seem to be demanding suicide, clearly it's time to check your premises.

Nathaniel Branden
Author, lecturer, and therapist—
A pioneer in the field of self-esteem and personal development

## SUICIDE

Generally, individuals commit suicide because they feel there is no other solution: *no hope!* Reasons could be financial or personal (relationship problem, low self-esteem etc.) or due to a mood disorder. A lack of purpose in life also adds to a feeling of futility. Countries with the highest suicide rates in the world are Russia, Lithuania, Belarus, Kazakhstan, Ukraine and Hungary. Belgium, Finland, Switzerland, Austria, France, and Japan have medium/high suicide rates. Denmark, Germany, China, Sweden, Australia, Canada, India and the US have medium suicide rates. Countries with the lowest suicide rates in the world are Muslim states together with Spain, Italy, Israel, Argentina, Brazil, Thailand and the UK.

### THE BOTTOM LINE
Your loved ones will suffer endlessly.

## SUICIDAL TENDENCIES

My fortune somewhat resembled that of a person who should entertain an idea of committing suicide, and, altogether beyond his hopes, meet with the good hap to be murdered.

Nathaniel Hawthorne (1804—64)
*The Custom House*

## SUICIDAL TENDENCIES

Can you imagine what it must be like for a parent to learn that their much-loved son or daughter—*who only a few months ago was full of the joys of life*—has committed suicide?

Adults and children who commit suicide are typically those who feel that death is the only way of escaping from what seems to them an impossible life without hope—*although, in some cases*—it is a cry for help that went unheeded.

The decision to commit suicide and the actions taken towards that end are invariably the consequences of negative thinking: the primary characteristic of depression. More people commit suicide today than die in road accidents. Lots of them are teenagers and young people.

### THE BOTTOM LINE

Cry for help or silence? *Think book!*

## SEASONAL AFFECTIVE DISORDER

Daylight reveals colour; artificial light drains it

Helena Rubinstein (1870—1965)
Polish cosmetics industrialist and the first self-made female millionaire

Escape from Depression / 69

## SEASONAL AFFECTIVE DISORDER

Often abbreviated to SAD, this is a type of depression with a seasonal pattern, occurring mostly in the winter months.

SAD is most common between the ages of 18—30 and sleep patterns, energy levels and mood may deteriorate in autumn and winter due to lack of daylight. Self-help solutions include:

- ☺ learn relaxation techniques
- ☺ leave major projects until spring
- ☺ get outside when possible
- ☺ sit near windows when inside
- ☺ decorate using light colours
- ☺ take regular, moderate exercise
- ☺ eat a well-balanced diet
- ☺ reduce the stress in your life
- ☺ light therapy is also effective.

<u>THE BOTTOM LINE</u>

Follow the *HAPPY FACES* guidelines.

## INTERNET BLUES

Modern man lives under the illusion
that he knows what he wants,
while he actually wants what he is
supposed to want.

Erich Fromm (1900—80)
*The Fear of Freedom*

## INTERNET BLUES

Are you hooked on the net? The internet can be an effortless expressway to enlightenment on any subject—*including 50,000+ sites dedicated to suicide*—clearly, not an ideal environment for the depressed! The internet can be a wonderful place to kick-start one's social life and find a new partner, but a recent study in America warns that too much exposure to the internet can induce loneliness, isolation and depression. The alternative? Live your life in the real world. We were born to *live*, not surf (unless there's an ocean around). The computer was designed to be our slave. Are we becoming enslaved by our computer toys?

### THE BOTTOM LINE
Avoid lingering in cyberspace.

## THE 'BABY BLUES' AND POSTNATAL DEPRESSION

Baby, sleep a little longer, till the little limbs are stronger.

Alfred, Lord Tennyson (1809-92)
*Sea Dreams*

## THE 'BABY BLUES' AND POSTNATAL DEPRESSION

These are two very different things. Let's address the easy one first. After the birth of a baby almost half of all mothers suffer a period of mild depression termed 'the blues'. This may last for a few hours or days and then it goes.

Postnatal depression is an illness that affects roughly 10% of new mothers and it can set in during the week of the birth and up to six months afterwards. There is a rare variation called postpartum psychosis affecting 0.1% of mothers and this requires urgent medical attention.

Many women feel worse just before, or during, a period. One solution can be progesterone therapy. Vitamin B6 or a general vitamin supplement often helps.

### THE BOTTOM LINE

You will prevail for your baby's sake.

## 'I'M A MAN: WE DON'T "DO" DEPRESSION'

"It's snowing still," said Eeyore gloomily.
"So it is."
"And freezing."
"Is it?"
"Yes," said Eeyore. "However," he said, brightening up a little, "we haven't had an earthquake lately."

A. A. Milne (1882—1956)
English author
*Winnie the Pooh*

## 'I'M A MAN: WE DON'T "DO" DEPRESSION'

Come on, guys, the game's up! When we are depressed we suffer every bit as much as women but because of our 'macho' mentality, we are less likely to admit it or seek help. And not without reason: this traditionally tough and self-reliant view of how men should behave is still revered by some women.

According to the Royal College of Psychiatrists in Britain in their admirable booklet titled *Men Behaving Sadly*, men are around three times more likely than women to kill themselves. Many men, when they recover from depression (as everyone does providing they don't do anything irreversible) emerge stronger.

### THE BOTTOM LINE
Get real; admit how you feel.

## DEPRESSION IN TERMINAL ILLNESS

Can I see another's woe?
And not be in sorrow too.
Can I see another's grief?
And not seek for kind relief.

William Blake (1757—1827)
*Songs of Innocence*

## DEPRESSION IN TERMINAL ILLNESS

We all die someday, but why do some patients recover from critical conditions when their doctors believe there is no hope of recovery?

Bernie Siegel, the American physician and author of *Love, Medicine and Miracles*, observed decades ago that patients who were ultimately successful in recovering from advanced stages of cancer had been described by doctors and nursing staff as difficult patients.

I know this to be true from my own determined efforts to make a complete recovery from the ravages of stroke. Prof. Sir Peter Morris, my surgeon, wrote about me: *'He was extremely angry about this (stroke) and unavoidably showed this in his relationships with his carers.'* OK, Sorry. But I got better.

---

### THE BOTTOM LINE

Some patients defy doctors' predictions.

## ANGER

Do not teach your children never to be angry; teach them how to be angry.

Lyman Abbot (1835—1922)
American Congregationalist,
theologian, editor and author

## ANGER

How dare some phantom from hell, in the space of a few brutal but painless moments, penetrate my brain, paralyzing my body on one side? What strange sadistic force, I wonder, would rearrange my face so that one corner of my mouth was an inconvenient inch higher than the other, and then transform *me*, an articulate person, into a babbling fool? Is this the devil's idea of fun? Angry about the strokes…? Yes!

Anger, directed and managed to perfection, is a potent weapon in the fight to recover from serious illness, and indeed from the perverseness of depression. Read on: in later pages I will reveal the secret of how some people harness the positive power of anger to defy all odds.

<u>THE BOTTOM LINE</u>
Harness the energy from your anger.

## HAPPINESS

We tend to forget that happiness doesn't come as a result of getting something we don't have, but rather of recognizing and appreciating what we do have.

Frederick "Fred" Koenig (1871—1950)
American wrestling champion

## HAPPINESS

I am a great admirer of Martin "Marty" Seligman, the American psychologist, author of self-help books and director of the Positive Psychology Centre at the University of Pennsylvania.

In his 2011 book, titled *Flourish: A New Understanding of Happiness and Well-Being—and How to Achieve Them* he

teaches that greater well-being is within our power. We think too much about what goes wrong in our lives and not enough about what goes right. He argues that we should savour what goes well and this brings me to my universal point of agreement with the great man: depressed people dwell on what is wrong in their lives; not what is right.

<u>THE BOTTOM LINE</u>
Positive approaches work.

## RETIRED EARLY, ON THE SCRAP HEAP, DEPRESSED

Any coward can sit in his home and criticize a pilot for flying into a mountain in fog. But I would rather, by far, die on a mountainside than die in bed. What kind of man would live where there is no daring?

Charles Lindbergh (1902—1974) "Lucky Lindy," as he was nick-named, was an American aviator who emerged from virtual obscurity to almost instantaneous world fame in 1927 by flying non-stop from New York to Paris. He later became a prolific prize-winning author.

## RETIRED EARLY, ON THE SCRAP HEAP, DEPRESSED

After my strokes and operations, I was transported down to Cornwall in the care of a loving niece to live out my days. Polperro, with its lovely people, laid-back lifestyle and abundance of pubs was welcoming and a real taste of Paradise. Nevertheless, I absconded over the River Tamar to Plymouth: a tough and challenging city 20 miles away in Devon. Why? I knew if I got used to the easy life, I would be finished.

The recipe for a happy early retirement is to bring to a close your previous working life (unless you can go on benefiting from it) and to be open to new possibilities. I have been living off my various disasters and fight backs since the beginning of the noughties!

### THE BOTTOM LINE
'Retirement' can be absolute bliss!

## **DEPRESSION <u>REQUIRING</u> SPECIALIST INTERVENTION**

I do not know whether I was then a man dreaming I was a butterfly, or whether I am now a butterfly dreaming I am a man.

Chuang-Tzu (396—289 BC)
Chinese philosopher

## DEPRESSION <u>REQUIRING</u> SPECIALIST INTERVENTION

The term 'clinical depression' is used to categorize any form of depression where symptoms are severe and long lasting.

☹ *Melancholic*: all interest in the activities of life is lost.

☺ *Manic-depressive psychosis*
☹ (bipolar disorder): alternating periods of extreme melancholia and equally extreme periods of elation.

☹ *Atypical depression*: persistent instead of periodic. Sufferers sensitive to romantic rejection.

☺ *Schizophrenia*: a serious mental
☹ illness that affects 1% of the population. Apparent in late teens or early twenties

BE SURE TO TAKE MEDICATIONS PRESCRIBED.

## **MCDAVID & BURGER-QUEEN**

If it has four legs and is not a chair, has wings and is not an aeroplane, or swims and is not a submarine, the Cantonese will eat it.

HRH Prince Philip, Duke of Edinburgh (b. 1921)

## MCDAVID & BURGER-QUEEN

My dilemma, as author and publisher is: do I tell the truth as I see it and risk the wrath of the food Goliaths, or do I keep quiet knowing that you might experience my fate? Well, my name's David...

I don't wish to be unkind to a burger chain that serves up delicious fare but I have irreversible arterial disease and I have a confession to make.

OK, so I used to be a smoker, but after the collapse of my second marriage and six months before the onset of two strokes, I moved to a new home situated temptingly close to a McDavid & Burger-Queen. Guess where I used to eat? Take special note of the next page and with no disrespect to Prince Philip, the Chinese eat a healthy diet!

<u>THE BOTTOM LINE</u>
If you can avoid it, *do it*!

88 / Slimline Secrets

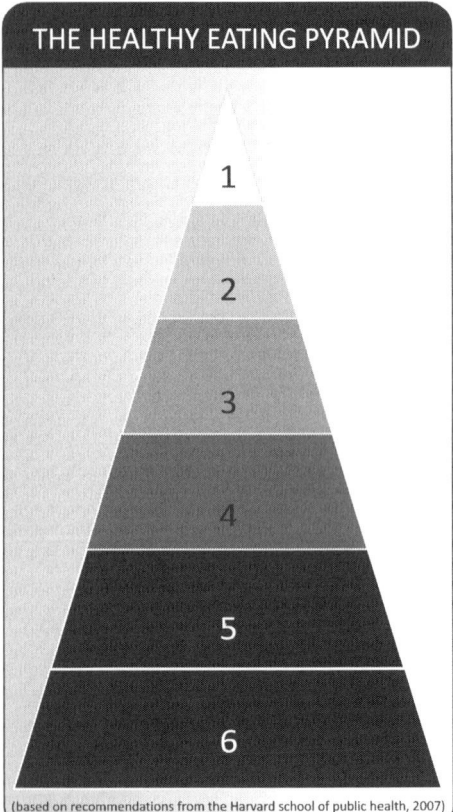

## THE HEALTHY EATING PYRAMID

1
2
3
4
5
6

(based on recommendations from the Harvard school of public health, 2007)

## THE HEALTHY EATING PYRAMID

1. Red meat
   butter
   white carbohydrates
   soda and sweets
   Used sparingly

2. Dairy: 1-2 times a day

3. Fish
   poultry
   eggs
   Up to 2 times a day

4. Nuts and legumes
   1-3 times a day

5. Vegetables—in abundance
   & fruit 2-3 times a day

6. Wholegrain foods
   and plant oils
   (olive, canola) frequently.

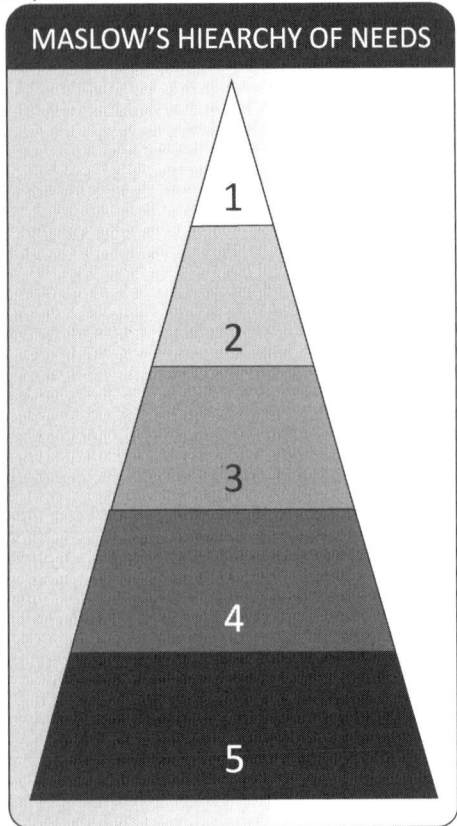

## MASLOW'S HIEARCHY OF NEEDS

1
2
3
4
5

## MASLOW'S HIEARCHY OF NEEDS

**1 Self-actualisation**
Growth, fulfilment
acceptance, creativity

**2 Esteem/status needs**
Achievement, responsibility
reputation, recognition

**3 Belonging/love needs**
Family, friendship
affection, work, relationship

**4 Safety needs**
Protection,
physical and financial security,
order stability

**5 Basic life needs**
Oxygen, nutrition,
water, shelter,
clothing, warmth, sleep

## TRAINING YOUR MIND

Let us train our minds to desire what the situation demands

Seneca (4 BC—AD 65)
Roman philosopher and statesman

## **TRAINING YOUR MIND**

The situation demands that we train our minds in preparation for our forthcoming escape from depression.

In the brief mind workouts (after the next section), we will learn how to control our thoughts, benefit from and then neutralize anger, tame fear, get active, sleep well, practise positive imagery, increase self-esteem and learn to forgive.

This experience will be enlightening and we shall approach it in easy stages, broken down into 10 palatable little chunks. To make solid progress, and to get value for money for the price you paid for this book, please participate in all the mind exercises and mini-assignments. They work! You benefit.

THE BOTTOM LINE
Grasp these gems and life gets better.

## **DUMPING EXCESS BAGGAGE**

How many things can I do without?

Socrates (c.470—399BC)
Classical Greek philosopher

## DUMPING EXCESS BAGGAGE

When escaping from depression, it is helpful to travel light and open up new channels of communication between mind, body and spirit.
In preparation for this adventure, it's worth checking to see how much excess baggage we have to jettison. The baggage I'm referring to is personal, very personal: those aspects of character that manifest themselves as bad habits, prejudices, negative thinking and self-destructive patterns of behaviour. Do you have any of these to get rid of?
When we've jettisoned the excess baggage and commenced the process of reconnecting your disconnected self, your depression will begin to lift.

<u>THE BOTTOM LINE</u>
Be done with the clutter.

## THOUGHT-STOPPING STRATEGIES

Life does not consist mainly—or even largely—of facts and happenings. It consists mainly of the storm of thoughts that are forever blowing through one's mind.

Mark Twain (1835—1910)
American author and humourist

## THOUGHT-STOPPING STRATEGIES

Let's discover how to stop, at will, the storm of thoughts blowing through our mind. The process is called 'SOS' after the internationally recognised distress code and it's also an abbreviation for the experiences I want you to enjoy: *silence, oblivion* and *serenity*.

To achieve success in SOS you should practise for 5 minutes a day over 30 days, commencing today. The types of thoughts we are going to target are those unwanted, negative and repetitive ones that drift into mind uninvited.

Find somewhere quiet where you will not be disturbed. Put your mobile to sleep and empty your mind of all thoughts for one beautiful moment. When thoughts invade, as they will to begin with, flick them out and start over.

<u>THE BOTTOM LINE</u>
Practise makes perfect: SOS! SOS! SOS!

## DESPERATION OR INSPIRATION?

In life you need either inspiration or desperation.

Tony Robbins (b.1960)
American self-help author and success coach

## DESPERATION OR INSPIRATION?

Referring to Tony's comments on the left, I assume we're short on inspiration, but high on desperation? I know I was when my life was decimated in a stroke.

From my hospital bed, fuming at God for doing the devil's work—*it didn't occur to me at that time that I might have been the architect of my own misfortune*—I used my desperation to speed my recovery. Every night, before I went off to sleep, I would kick and cajole my foot on the stroke-affected side of my body that wanted to drag in an invalid-like posture, into the pre-stroke position. Desperate?... I was frantic! I waged war on my body until it did what I wanted it to do. Is there some positive way you can exploit your desperation?

<u>THE BOTTOM LINE</u>
Use desperation to advantage.

## NEUTRALISING ANGER

Holding on to anger is like holding on
to a hot coal with the intent of
throwing it at someone else;
you are the one who gets burned.

Buddha (563 BC—483 BC)

## NEUTRALIZING ANGER

Holding on to anger when it can serve no useful purpose is dangerous to health. Suppressed or internalized anger can lead to high blood pressure. If someone has made you angry, or if you have angered somebody and you regret it, ask for, or offer an apology. If a partner is involved, try to make-up at or before bedtime. If this advice is just not feasible in the circumstances, release those angry emotions while dancing to music in the privacy of your home. Alternatively, write the offender the letter from hell. Only don't send it! Or try confronting the ugliness of anger in the mirror. Don't shy away! Hold your gaze. Any tears? Good! Already venom and anger are bailing out through the windows.

THE BOTTOM LINE
Sort it, bin it, and forget it.

## **TAMING FEAR**

There is no terror in a bang, only in the anticipation of it.

(Sir) Alfred Hitchcock (1899—1980)
British film director and producer

## TAMING FEAR

Taming fear! This sounds *scary*. Living with a sensible level of fear, to prevent our walking across the street without looking, is part of our survival instinct. But irrational fear can be paralyzing and render us vulnerable to panic attacks and phobias. Sufferers should seek one-to-one counselling.

The American psychologist and author of the book, *Feel the Fear and Do It Anyway*, was right all along. We have to accept that when we try new and different things it can get a little bit scary. We might momentarily experience a pounding heart and get sweaty palms. So what? When we carry on regardless and do what we fear most; the chances are that next time we won't be afraid

### THE BOTTOM LINE
Many fears are tissue-paper thin. Blow!

## GETTING ACTIVE

Action is consolatory. It is the enemy of thought and the friend of flattering illusions.

Joseph Conrad (1857—1924)
Polish-born English novelist

## GETTING ACTIVE

The most obvious sign of depression is that we become less active. Everything seems to be such a chore and since we get little or no satisfaction from what we do, we unwittingly make things worse by doing very little, allowing ourselves to become stagnant.

Many years ago, when I was depressed, having lost my health and my business empire, I remember thinking more about the past than living each day and planning for the future. I was so exhausted from all this reminiscing that action was out of the question. *This is wrong!* Exercise is essential for recovery. The key to progress is to take a little exercise each day, commencing today... A walk in the park is a great place to start.

### THE BOTTOM LINE

Just look at the benefits over the page!

## STAYING ACTIVE

Those people who think they have no time or inclination for physical exercise will sooner or later have to make time for illness.

Author unknown

Escape from Depression / 107

## STAYING ACTIVE

Unless you are medically unfit, aim to get yourself a little breathless when working out. *Exercise is effective in*:

1. Clearing our minds
2. Reducing insomnia
3. Improving muscle tone
4. Rejuvenating immune system
5. Improving digestion
6. Stimulating blood flow
7. Regenerating skeletal joints
8. Building up stamina
9. Decreasing cholesterol levels
10. Lowering blood pressure
11. Strengthening heart and lungs
12. Cleansing our emotional systems
13. Toning our respiratory system
14. Preventing heart disease
15. Burning calories
16. Escaping from depression

## QUALITY SLEEP

God bless the inventor of sleep, the cloak that covers all men's thoughts, the food that cures all hunger... the balancing weight that levels the shepherd with the king.

Miguel Cervantes (1547—1616) Spanish novelist, poet, and playwright (*Don Quixote* is regarded as the first modern novel and a classic of Western literature)

## QUALITY SLEEP

The most wonderful thing about quality sleep is the joy of waking up refreshed. Sadly, this is seldom the experience of the depressed person. To aid quality sleep, take some exercise during the day. I find listening to soothing classical music is effective; some find a hot bath helps; many prepare for sleep by making love to their partner or walking the dog. Cocoa or hot chocolate is the elixir of sleep for many. Coffee is not advisable. Avoid drinking too much alcohol: it might help you to fall asleep but you are likely to wake up in the night.

If something is troubling you and you can't deal with it before retiring, note it down for action tomorrow, and go to bed with a clear conscience.

### THE BOTTOM LINE
Establish your routine for bedtime.

## SELF-ESTEEM

When people believe in themselves
they have the first secret of success.

Norman Vincent Peale (1898—1993)
*The Power of Positive Thinking*

## SELF-ESTEEM

In your dreams you are able to do some remarkable things. You can be in two different places at the same time, walk through walls, get along with friends and associates and have passionate affairs with whomever you please. You can do all these things and more in your dreams because you don't doubt yourself. Doubt is the arch-enemy of self-esteem and in order to believe in yourself you must accept you are gifted in a unique way. When you get right down to it, people with high self-esteem are men and women who are comfortable and at peace with themselves. They are happy with the way their lives are progressing regardless of whether they are serving drinks or writing bestsellers.

<u>THE BOTTOM LINE</u>

*Believe* you are gifted in a unique way.

## **GREATER SELF-ESTEEM**

There's only one corner of the universe you can be certain of improving, and that's your own self.

Aldous Huxley (1894—1963)
*Time Must Have a Stop*

## GREATER SELF-ESTEEM

Stand tall and proud in front of a mirror and say the following words with authority, sincerity and conviction:

"I AM A GOOD PERSON. I VALUE MYSELF."

Look yourself straight in the face; say it again. And again! Do this every day for 30 days. *Don't miss out one single day*.

It might be a good idea to make sure nobody is around at the time because we are not interested in anyone else's opinion; only our own. Also, try putting these practical guidelines to good effect.

- Avoid being stand-offish
- Sit/stand where you can be seen
- Introduce yourself to others
- Smile! The action of smiling, even if it's not sincere at the outset, actually lifts your mood.

<u>THE BOTTOM LINE</u>
I like being me.

## DEFAULT SETTINGS OF YOUR MIND

We know what we are, but we know not what we may be.

William Shakespeare (1564—1616)
*Hamlet*

## DEFAULT SETTINGS OF YOUR MIND

To make this crucial point supremely easy to understand, I am going to use the analogy between the human mind and a computer. For those of us who are not computer buffs, I should point out that if a computer is programmed to do something, it will go on doing that thing until you instruct it to do otherwise.

For instance, if the space setting on your computer is pre-set to leave two spaces after a full stop, that is what you will get unless the setting is altered to leave only one space. Parallel this with a depressed person whose thought patterns have a tendency to be negative and it is clear we need to re-program the default settings of the mind from negative to positive to get well.

<u>THE BOTTOM LINE</u>
One change of mind will do it.

**D-THOUGHTS**

Great thoughts come from the heart.

Marquis de Vauvenargues (1715—47)
French moralist and writer

## D-THOUGHTS

The all-important fact to grasp in this section is this:

D = depression and
D-THOUGHTS = thoughts that will lead you into depression in the first place and keep you trapped in depression until something changes.

The main contributing factor in almost all depressive illnesses and suicides is negative thinking—D-thoughts!

In a little while I am going to teach you a simple method for neutralizing D-thoughts and reprogramming the default settings of your mind so that you can be more positive about recovery.

<u>THE BOTTOM LINE</u>
D-thoughts are depressing thoughts.

## THE REVISED DEFAULT SETTING FOR PEACE OF MIND

Great emergencies and crises show us how much greater our vital resources are than we had supposed.

William James (1842—1910)
Psychologist and philosopher

## THE REVISED DEFAULT SETTING FOR PEACE OF MIND

D-thoughts are thoughts that condition us to expect the worse and they deprive us of so many of the joys of life. They are self-deprecating thoughts that spring to mind instantaneously if you let them.
The time is approaching for you reclaim ownership of your own mind and stop D-thoughts in their tracks. Are you ready?
Actually, you may find that you are already well on your way to revising the default settings of your mind. The SOS exercise I set you for five minutes a day over 30 days in the *THOUGHT-STOPPING STRATEGIES* section earlier is a warm up procedure for the next section. Have you done your homework?

<u>THE BOTTOM LINE</u>
It's time to graduate from SOS to Ss30.

## SS30

Human beings, who are almost unique in having the ability to learn from the experience of others, are also remarkable for their apparent disinclination to do so.

Douglas Adams (1952—2001)
English writer and dramatist best known for *The Hitchhiker's Guide to the Galaxy*

## SS30

**SS30** **S**top! Every time you catch yourself thinking a negative, depression-inducing D-thought, *dismiss it from mind*. Flick it out and think of something pleasing or positive fast.

**SS30** **S**uspend disbelief in the effectiveness of this process for a period of 30 days. If you follow these instructions faithfully for 30 days you will have won. It will have worked.

**SS30** **30** days is how long it can take to make or break a habit. Don't worry if you find it tricky at first. It gets easier, much easier.

SS30: DO IT AND YOU ESCAPE DEPRESSION.

## THERAPEUTIC THOUGHTS

Our life is what our thoughts make it.

Marcus Aurelius (AD 121—180)
Roman Emperor for the years
161—180

## THERAPEUTIC THOUGHTS

*The way we think in turn affects our emotions and thus our behaviour.*

Please go back over the opening sentence and read it again. Do you really understand what it means? Do you recognize the implications of that one sentence? It means you can be depression-free just by persevering with SS30 and doing this simple exercise that works every day until you are happy.

***Exercise***: Jot down 3 things that made you happy today. Keep thinking until you find them, no matter how minor they may be. No excuses! Do it every day.

Incidentally, those opening words of wisdom came from none other than the brilliant Aaron T. Beck. He is an American psychiatrist and a professor emeritus at the University of Pennsylvania.

<u>THE BOTTOM LINE</u>
Treat yourself to some nice thoughts.

## THE TALKING THERAPIES

Conversation has a kind of charm about it, an insinuating and insidious something that elicits secrets from us just like love or liquor.

Seneca (4 BC—AD 65)
Roman philosopher and advisor to Emperor Nero

## THE TALKING THERAPIES

Every depressed person needs someone sympathetic to talk to. This person may be a friend, family member, work colleague, or a professional from the caring professions. If you are lucky enough to have an empathetic hairdresser, they too can be helpful.

Actually finding such a person, someone who really understands, is incredibly comforting and empowering. GP surgeries and libraries can normally point you in the right direction.

In those rare moments when we feel able to give voice to our confused and despairing thoughts, the greatest gift we can hope for is to have someone with the capacity to listen; and to show us—with especial sensitivity—the next step forward.

THE BOTTOM LINE

Professional therapy can enrich your life.

## **THE ULTIMATE CHALLENGE: FORGIVENESS**

The weak can never forgive. Forgiveness is the attribute of the strong.

Mahatma Gandhi (1869—1948)
Prominent figure of the Indian independence movement

## THE ULTIMATE CHALLENGE: FORGIVENESS

I wish I had read and heeded the quote from Gandhi, opposite, earlier in life. I left home at 15 with no qualifications after a major quarrel with my father. It was ten years before I forgave my mother and my father died before I *truly* forgave him. What was their crime? They failed to be the perfect parents! I feel so ashamed and weak but as least I did the right thing in the end; albeit too late for my father.

*Do you have any unfinished business*? If so, brace yourself for a revelation! The quotation that follows may not be beautiful, but it is telling. It could be the key to your escape from depression.

<u>THE BOTTOM LINE</u>
Will you be strong or weak?

## FORGIVENESS: *PREPARING FOR IT!*

To forgive is to set a prisoner free and discover the prisoner was you.

Lewis B. Smedes (1921—2002)
Professor of theology and ethics at Fuller Theological Seminary in Pasadena, California, and author

Escape from Depression / 129

## FORGIVENESS: *PREPARING FOR IT!*

If, like me, you are in shock and awe at Professor Smedes' words of wisdom and undeniable truth—*THAT'S GOOD*—we can sort it! I'll show you what to do and how to do it. You will do the rest. You must. We're in this together: your recovery matters—my reputation is at stake here.

Incidentally, it might surprise you to know that in my consultancy I learned that sometimes the person that needed to be forgiven was the depressed client, the one who was paying my fees.

As a kid at school, I never did quite get the meaning of The Lord's Prayer from the Book of Common Prayer: *And forgive us our trespasses, as we forgive them that trespass against us*. I do now.

<u>THE BOTTOM LINE</u>
Forgive and forget.

## FORGIVENESS: *WHAT IF I'M NOT READY?*

As long as you *DON'T* forgive, who and whatever it is will occupy rent-free space in your mind.

Isabelle Holland (1920—2002)
Swiss author of children's and adult fiction living in England and America

## FORGIVENESS: *WHAT IF I'M NOT READY?*

Are you quite sure you don't want to get yourself ready? Grief! When I think of my sins of neglect as a father to my son living in Thailand, my daughter conceived in London and born in Stockholm, and my Oriental daughter living in Milton Keynes, I wonder how on earth I had the nerve to criticize and condemn my own parents who at least stuck together for the sake of the family.

Clearly, I have put myself through the process of forgiveness that I commend to you and have come to terms with my own failings. I am no longer depressed. However, if you are not ready or able to forgive, I respect your special reasons.

### THE BOTTOM LINE
If you can't or won't forgive, for pity's sake, *dismiss them from mind!*

## FORGIVENESS: *THINKING ABOUT IT!*

There is no revenge as complete as forgiveness.

Josh Billings (1818—1885)
American humourist and writer

## FORGIVENESS: *THINKING ABOUT IT!*

What is forgiveness? Before we do it—*because this is for real and for ever and will be pivotal in your escape from depression*—let's be clear what is forgiveness. It is the cancellation of an emotional debt from the wrongdoer to you; and/or, perhaps, from you to you.

Depressed people can have particular difficulty in achieving reconciliation after experiencing hostility, regardless of whether the hurt occurred one month or fifty years before.

People find it so hard to forgive because they need to be proved right, to possess the moral high ground, the dominant position. I fell into that trap before I figured out that the one who heals the rift—*regardless of right or wrong*—could be the finer character.

<u>THE BOTTOM LINE</u>
Get ready.

## FORGIVENESS: THE BASIC PRINCIPLES

Rules are not necessarily sacred,
principles are.

Franklin D. Roosevelt (1882—1945)
The 32nd President of the United States

## FORGIVENESS: THE BASIC PRINCIPLES

Before we forgive others, don't forget to forgive yourself: life didn't come with a step-by-step instruction manual! There are 3 straightforward steps to forgiveness:

**STEP 1** Dissolving resentment

**STEP 2** Identifying with the wrongdoer's possible motivation in a compassionate (or, if that is impossible) non-judgemental way

**STEP 3** The act of forgiveness itself, which is forever irretrievable. You can't wake up tomorrow and decide to rescind your forgiveness. Please note, the sequence and execution of these exorcisms are exactly the same regardless of whether you are forgiving yourself or other people.

## **FORGIVENESS: *DOING IT!***

To err is human, to forgive, divine.

Alexander Pope (1688—1744)
English poet

## FORGIVENESS: *DOING IT!*

**STEP 1** Dissolve your resentment. Decide first if you would prefer to visualize this scene in your mind, paint, draw, write or create it on your computer. See the person you are going to forgive sitting, standing, or kneeling before you. Make them feel at ease.

**STEP 2** Identify with the wrongdoer's possible motivation in a compassionate or non-judgemental way. Try to see things from their perspective.

**STEP 3** The act of forgiveness. Say the name of the person and then forgive them generously and completely once-and-for-all. It is not necessary or advisable to forgive them in person but you can if you prefer. *There, it's done!*

WHEN YOU WAKE UP TOMORROW, A HEAVY WEIGHT FROM YOUR MIND WILL BE LIFTED.

## SWIMMING WITH DOLPHINS

If I could get any animal it would be a dolphin. I want one so bad. Me and my mom went swimming with dolphins and I was like, 'How do we get one of those?' and she was like, 'You can't get a dolphin. What are you gonna do, like, put it in your pool?'

Miley Cyrus (1992—)
American actress and pop singer

## SWIMMING WITH DOLPHINS

Morab, an Arab living in Israel, was a popular high school student, until he sent an innocent text message to a girl in his class. The girl's family, deciding that the message was 'inappropriate', beat him to the brink of death.

Morab was left with post-traumatic dissociation and was unable to speak or communicate until his father took him to Eilat on the Red Sea for 'dolphin therapy' according to a mesmerizing TV documentary in 2011. Many depressed clients have reported benefits in swimming with dolphins. Horace Dobbs, a former atomic scientist, reports that their brains have the ability to carry out ultrasonic scans, which makes them sensitive to human emotions.

### THE BOTTOM LINE
If you can swim and afford it, *try it*!

## MUSIC THERAPY

For me, singing sad songs often has a way of healing a situation. It gets the hurt out in the open into the light, out of the darkness.

Reba McEntire (b.1955)
American country music singer and actress

## MUSIC THERAPY

Music possesses that special quality capable of making us aware of our innermost feelings. Somehow it becomes acceptable to shed tears while listening to a sad or moving song.

The right music can have an extraordinarily powerful effect in exploring and exposing the hidden motivations for our darkest moods and most private melancholy. It can function as a catalyst for discovering, soothing and disentangling deep-rooted sadness and internal mayhem. It can be therapeutic and mood enhancing to listen to sad and lethargic music, followed by something moody, changeable, mid-tempo, before ending on an upbeat, happy, electrifying note.

THE BOTTOM LINE
We are all touched by music.

## DANCE THERAPY

Please send me your last pair of shoes, worn out with dancing as you mentioned in your letter, so that I might have something to press against my heart.

Johann Wolfgang von Goethe
(1749—1832)
German writer considered by many to be the supreme genius of modern German literature.

## DANCE THERAPY

Dance is one of the oldest therapies known to man and yet it is only recently that dance has become an accepted therapeutic tool.

Dance has the capability to lift dulled and depressed individuals out of their everyday tedium and to get their underactive bodies moving and stretching in time to the music. To a large extent, it does away with the necessity for one to think or talk. Dance allows many alienated people to come together in a social environment as well as being an effective therapeutic tool.

Getting the depressed person out into this therapeutic environment is a problem in itself; and a task for friends

### THE BOTTOM LINE
We're fools whether we dance or not, so we might as well dance...
*Japanese proverb*

## **PET THERAPY**

Animals are such agreeable friends—they ask no questions, they pass no criticisms.

George Eliot (1819—80)
*Scenes of Clerical Life*

## PET THERAPY

For some people, acquiring a pet can be the beginning of a magical partnership, and the act of ownership can mark the end of depressive illness.

In Britain alone, around seven million canine chums now share human homes and no fewer than eight million purring moggies are currently providing their owners with snug companionship.

Just having a pet around has been shown to reduce stress and improve the owner's general sense of wellbeing. Cats and dogs are more than man's best friend. Studies have shown that pets can help their owners in a variety of ways, including the lowering of blood pressure, improving mood and speeding recovery from depression.

### THE BOTTOM LINE
If you are all alone, why not get a pet?

## MASSAGE

I like a man what takes his time.

Mae West (1892—1980)
American actress and sex symbol

## MASSAGE

One of the great joys of massage is that you are helpless on the massage couch with nothing to do. You have little choice but to lie back and let your masseur or masseuse do with you as they think fit.

Massage releases tension, alleviates some types of headache, frees energy, soothes aching muscles and makes you feel good. It also brings awareness to the sensory nerves—just what you need when you are feeling dulled and depressed.

Should you find yourself thinking negatively or worrying about something, remember your D-thought training in SOS. Flick it out of mind and relax, revelling in the unparalleled luxury of being pampered in the name of therapy!

THE BOTTOM LINE
Touch can help to heal.

## SEX IN DEPRESSION

If you use the electric vibrator near
water, you will come and go
at the same time

Louise Sammons
aboutmylovequotes.com

## SEX IN DEPRESSION

Many people live happily without an active sex life, but for others, a satisfying sex life can be an important part of health and wellbeing. At the moment of climax, your brainwaves are being well and truly scrambled. This enjoyable sensation is not altogether different from the therapeutic benefits that can be derived from a less popular choice of therapy—ECT (electric shock treatment)!

Problems of a sexual nature in depression include:

- Difficulty in becoming aroused
- Reduced sexual performance
- Realizing less pleasure
- Less inclination
- Difficulty with erection
- Premature or non-ejaculation
- Loss of desire; vaginal dryness

THE BOTTOM LINE
These problems are only temporary.

## HOT BATHS AND MIND GAMES

It is the height of luxury to sit in a hot bath and read about little birds...

Lord Alfred Tennyson (1809—92) British Poet Laureate during much of Queen Victoria's reign, upon having hot water installed in his new house

## **HOT BATHS AND MIND GAMES**

Some people haven't taken a bath for years! In this high-tech, energy-efficient age, millions of people miss out on the therapeutic benefits of a hot, leisurely bath in preference to a quick shower.

Edmund Wilson, the noted US writer and critic, had this to say about my favourite early morning routine: 'I have had a great many more uplifting thoughts, creative and expansive visions while soaking in comfortable baths in well-equipped American bathrooms than I have ever had in any cathedral.'

Can I not tempt you into a luxuriously long and uninterrupted hot bath, complete with the aroma of mind-soothing geranium and rosewood? Don't forget your soft, fluffy towel!

### THE BOTTOM LINE

*Slimline Secrets* were conceived in a leisurely hot bath.

## A PURPOSE IN LIFE

Nothing contributes so much to tranquillise the mind as a steady purpose: a point on which the soul may fix its intellectual eye.

Mary Shelley (1797—1851)
British novelist and dramatist best known for *Frankenstein*

## A PURPOSE IN LIFE

Money, power, freedom, a huge and impressive home, the hunkiest, most handsome man imaginable to satisfy your every whim or the queen of the catwalks as your personal trophy. If you had all that, and more, would you be guaranteed to be free of depression? Actually, no: very rich and powerful people also sometimes get depressed.

The fastest way to escape from depression is to discover your purpose in life and then live the dream: *do it*! Everyone has a purpose in life and everybody can discover theirs if they probe deep enough. My purpose is to write and publish books that will improve the quality of your life. What is your purpose? *Shall we find out*?

THE BOTTOM LINE
In the West, destiny is a matter of
***choice***

## REALIZING YOUR PURPOSE

Life is not lost by dying; life is lost minute by minute, day by dragging day, in all the thousand small uncaring ways.

Stephen Vincent Benet (1898—1943) American author and poet: winner of a Pulitzer Prize in 1929

## **REALIZING YOUR PURPOSE**

This could be the most exciting breakthrough of your life. The process is simple and consists of 3 parts; the first 2 of which we'll deal with here:

1. *Decide*! What is it you want to do with the rest of your life? What would make your life meaningful, happy and fulfilled?
2. Once you've decided (this might take 10 seconds, 10 weeks or longer) put it to the *love test*!

What is the love test? Do you want it enough to do it for nothing—without being paid—if you had to? Of course you expect to make money, but if material benefit is the sole motive for your purpose, you are kidding yourself. Think again! Part 3 comes later.

<u>THE BOTTOM LINE</u>
Get this right and life is beautiful.

## CLARIFYING YOUR PURPOSE

I felt as if I were walking with destiny, and that my past life had been but a preparation for this hour and this trial... I was sure I should not fail.

Winston Churchill (1874-1965)

## CLARIFYING YOUR PURPOSE

Life has more meaning and depth to it when we have something definite to do—a mission to fulfil. If we fail to realize this we run the risk of getting lost and becoming depressed should we experience bad luck, disappointment or go through a period of forced change.

Many people start off with a passion for life but they lose it along the way. What really does it for you... painting, homemaking, TV, the armed forces, the chance to run your own business or the privilege of caring for others? The choices are endless.

If you spend your life doing what you love doing, it stands to reason that life will be a pleasure and you will excel at what you do.

<u>THE BOTTOM LINE</u>
Have the courage of your conviction.

## COMMITTING YOUR PURPOSE TO PAPER: THE MISSION STATEMENT

So the vision of Microsoft is pretty simple. For the first 25 years of the company, it was a personal computer on every desk and in every home.

Bill Gates (b.1955)
American entrepreneur and founder of Microsoft

## COMMITTING YOUR PURPOSE TO PAPER: THE MISSION STATEMENT

Bill Gates had a mission plan based on his vision for Microsoft and so should the rest of us. I want you to commit your purpose in life to paper in the form of a mission statement. It's a powerful way of concentrating your mind on what needs to happen. Make it brief and honest like the one I wrote below:

### David M Hinds
#### My life in the year 2000 and beyond

I am creative and will write some more motivational and self-help books. I am doing this with my life because I want to and I get satisfaction from what I write.

This year I will endeavour to find someone to love and cherish: someone who will love me forever. I will be truthful, kind and faithful to her and we will be friends as well as lovers and lifelong partners.

## LOVE

There is more hunger for love and appreciation in this world than there is for bread.

Mother Teresa (1910—1997)
Catholic nun of Albanian ethnicity and Indian citizenship—Nobel Peace Prize winner in 1997 for her humanitarian work with the poor and helpless

## LOVE

Why do some people find their ideal partner while others stagger from one broken relationship to the next or live their life alone? What enables some couples to have loving relationships that last while others end up on the rocks?

I think, at last, I have discovered the answers to these ambiguities of love. No space to clarify things here, but I assure you true love can and always will be found in the bleakest of circumstances.

After losing everything except my sanity and my friends—health, homes, money, *gone at a stroke*—I found the woman of my dreams and after 10 years of happy marriage we are deeply in love.

### THE BOTTOM LINE
Never give up hope of finding love.

## ENJOYING THE MOMENT

Happy the man, and happy he alone,
He, who can call to-day his own;
He, who, secure within, can say,
To-morrow do thy worst, for I have lived today.

John Dryden (1631—1700)
English poet, critic, and translator
From a translation of Horace (65—8 BC)

## ENJOYING THE MOMENT

OK, so you have embarked upon perhaps the most radical self-improvement programme of your life. This is brave of you and wise. Assuming you connect with the various exercises, participating in them and fully completing the programme, you will escape from depression and be much happier and more fulfilled as a result. If you've read this book right through from the beginning, I should imagine you are beginning to feel better already. By now you must know there is hope for you and plenty of good times and opportunities ahead.

But are you enjoying the experience? *Are you enjoying the moment*?

### THE BOTTOM LINE
Enjoy the moment. Every moment is precious.

## HIGHLIGHTING

Some books are to be tasted, others to be swallowed, and some few to be chewed and digested.

Francis Bacon (1561—1626)
English lawyer, politician, essayist and philosopher

## HIGHLIGHTING

You have done well! You've reached the last page but one and I wouldn't be surprised if this little book has proved quite a challenge! I sincerely hope *Slimline Secrets: Escape from Depression* delivers for you in the days, weeks or months ahead. There is a lot you can do to make sure it does!

Start by going back through the book and marking with a yellow highlighting pen those passages that resonate with you. Then work through the exercises to make sure you haven't missed out! Here at *Slimline Secrets* we are happy to receive feedback from readers although we regret we cannot reply. Please address any comments to: The Editor, Slimline Secrets UK, Unit 12, Monroe Gardens, Plymouth PL3 4GY.

### THE BOTTOM LINE
Just one more exercise to go! Bless you.

## THE DOOR IS OPEN
## AND THE JAILER WISHES YOU WELL...

Why do you stay in prison
when the door is so wide open?

Jalal al-Din Rumi
Supreme Persian poet and sage
(1207—1273)

Escape from Depression / 167

## MY RESOLUTION

My name is

..............................................

From now on my purpose in life is

..............................................

..............................................

Now that I have read *Slimline Secrets* I am going to

..............................................

..............................................

The help I need most is

..............................................

..............................................

## TRUST, NEGATIVE FEEDBACK, SELF BELIEF AND UNIQUENESS

Trust is like a mirror, you can fix it if it's broken, but you can still see the crack in that mother fucker's reflection...

Well, that's your opinion, isn't it? And I'm not about to waste my time trying to change it...

I had a boyfriend who told me I'd never succeed, never be nominated for a Grammy, never have a hit song...

You have to be unique, and different, and shine in your own way.

Lady Gaga (b.1986)

## *SLIMLINE SECRETS* OF SUCCESS

Conventional wisdom suggests that if and when we find success, we will be happy. Misguided! Happiness comes from within and, together with ambition and willpower, it fuels success, not the other way round.

In this concise and pleasurable book, David M Hinds offers *how to* tips that really hit home in the harsh reality of everyday life, making success possible.

Not everyone can achieve mega-success, but we can all significantly improve the quality of our lives, our contentment, and our future prospects by tapping into these powerful and easy to grasp strategies. This title delivers a motivational learning experience that shows readers how to get precisely what they want.

**NEW TITLE**

## *SLIMLINE SECRETS* QUIT SMOKING

The author has successfully steered UK clients to non-smoker status, on a face-to-face basis in his consultancy.

After years of enjoying cigarettes and, incidentally, six months before suffering a stroke from a blocked artery, he gave up his 60-a-day habit and has never smoked since. He knows the pitfalls and traps waiting for smokers bold enough to stub out and starve their nicotine habit.

Readers who follow the explicit instructions faithfully will give up the habit permanently and they will do so without wasting money on spurious nicotine patches or other paraphernalia. Make no mistake: giving up smoking is a challenge. But armed with this book, you can do it!

**NEW TITLE**

## BOUNCING BACK FROM FAILURE

This book is bursting with pick-yourself-up-and-go-power on the merits of taking a tumble and falling flat on your face. Failure is a cruel teacher but she is an awe-inspiring one. Readers are left in no doubt that success is the next *but one* stop on from failure. The extra step is crucial!

Of course, the would-be entrepreneur, the spurned lover, the disappointed - exhausted from their efforts - can't see the opportunity fate has handed them.

Readers are treated to dollops of TLC and a host of inspirational strategies to get them back on track to wherever they want to be. We all have our share of setbacks and failures. We all deserve this uplift.

**NEW TITLE**

## SLIMLINE SECRETS: GET WELL SOON

This warmly personal and patient-friendly book by an author who has experienced serious ill-health and recovered, addresses the needs of people who are not well with imagination, insight and empathy.

Not only will it have the effect of making the patient feel better, but the individual little nuggets of wisdom coalesce to form a practical step-by-step recovery plan.

Suitable for all ages and patients, this uplifting little book is positive, fun and thought-provoking. It makes an ideal gift for anyone ill in hospital or at home and it is far more practical than a bunch of grapes!

**NEW TITLE**

Escape from Depression / 173

## *SLIMLINE SECRETS* OF LOVE

Why do some people find their ideal partner while others stagger from one broken relationship to the next or live their life alone? What enables some couples to have loving relationships that last while others collapse?

Unlike all previous love and relationship books, David M Hinds tells it like it really is out there in the real world. His first two marriages ended in divorce so he certainly knows how not to do things! But he also knows with absolutely certainty you true love can be found and nourished in the bleakest of circumstances. After losing everything save his sanity and his friends—health, homes, money—*gone at a stroke*; he found the woman of my dreams and after 10 years of happy marriage they are very much in love.

**FORTHCOMING TITLE**

## EFFECTIVE COMPLAINING

We British—brilliant at war with an enviable civil rights record—are wimpish at complaining! We just don't know how to do it without feeling embarrassed or blowing a fuse.

The author—who has received £28,430 in cash, goods and benefits in kind from companies who short-changed him in the 3 year run-up to this book—shows readers how to take control and get tangible results.

House builders, hotels, high street banks, golf clubs, restaurants, supermarkets and utility companies... they were all made to pay up and apologise. Don't settle for a finger in your face, a voucher, or a bottle of plonk when things go wrong. Acquire the secrets of effective complaining.

### FORTHCOMING TITLE